There once was a tot
whose name was Scot.
He had a dog whose name was Spot.

They lived together in a flowerpot,
the tot named Scot and his good dog Spot.

2

The girl who lived next door to Scot
teased him for living in a flowerpot.
But this didn't bother Scot one jot—
he liked his home an awful lot.

There once was a tot
whose name was Dot.
She had a cat named Apricot.

They lived together in a big teapot,
the tot named Dot and sweet Apricot.

The boy who lived next door to Dot
teased her for living in a big teapot.
But this didn't bother Dot one jot—
she liked her home an awful lot.

One day when Scot was walking Spot,
he passed right by the big teapot.
"I love your house!" Scot told Dot.
(As a matter of fact, so did Spot!)

Then Scot told Dot, right on the spot,
all about his home in the flowerpot.

"I love your house!" Dot told Scot.
(As a matter of fact, so did Apricot!)

Now, when the weather is sunny and hot,
Dot visits Scot in his flowerpot.
They plant petunias and forget-me-nots.
(Apricot and Spot help out a lot!)

On chilly days, Scot visits Dot
for tea and cake in the big teapot.

The kids who once teased them,
now do not.

They wish they had homes
like Scot and Dot!

-ot Word Family Riddles

Listen to the riddle sentences. Add the right letter or letters to the -ot sound to finish each one.

1 We planted the daisies in a flower ____ot.

2 In the winter it is cold. In the summer it is ____ot.

3 Scot says his tea really "hits the ____ot!"

4 My mom said she liked my drawing a ____ot.

5 To tie a bow I must first tie a ____ot.

6 The clown's white shirt had one pink polka ____ot.

7 Cats climb trees, but dogs do ____ot.

8 The peach is a week old and has started to ____ot.

9 Horses can gallop and they can ____ot.

10 When the package arrived I shouted, "Look what I ____ot!"

Now make up some new riddle sentences using - ot

-ot

Give a great holler, a cheer, a yell

For all of the words that we can spell

With an O and a T that make the sound –ot,

You'll find it in hot and pot and Scot.

Two little letters, that's all that we need

To make a whole family of words to read.

Make a list of other –ot words. Then use them in the cheer!